THE TWO SOULS OF THE MANICHEANS

St. Augustine
Bishop of Hippo Regius

Translated by: D.P. Curtin

Copyright @ 2011 Dalcassian Press

All rights reserved. No part of this publication may be reproduced, distributed, or transmitted in any form or by any means, including photocopying, recording, or other electronic or mechanical methods, without the prior written permission of the publisher, except in the case of brief quotations embodied in critical reviews and certain other non-commercial uses permitted by copyright law. For permission request, write to Dalcassian Press at dalcassianpublishing at gmail.com

ISBN: 979-8-8693-9676-1 (Paperback)

Library of Congress Control Number:
Author: Curtin, D.P. (1985-)

Printed by Ingram Content Group, 1 Ingram Blvd, La Vergne, Tennessee

First printing edition 2011.

THE TWO SOULS OF THE MANICHEANS

The error of the Manichaeans concerning two souls, the other of which is not from God, is attacked by what argument. Every soul, since there is a kind of life, can only be from God as the source of life.

1. Relying on God's mercy, having broken and abandoned the traps of the Manichaeans, I would like to consider myself at last restored to the bosom of Catholicism, and to deplore my misery. For there were many things that I had to do, lest so easily and in a few days, the truest seeds of religion, healthily planted in me from my childhood, be driven from my heart by the error or fraud of false and deceitful men. For in the first place those two classes of souls, to whom they have given each their own natures, so that the one is of the very substance of God, but of the other they would not accept God or even the creator, if I had considered with myself soberly and diligently, with a mind devoted to God and pious; perhaps it would have appeared to me at first sight that there is no life of any kind which does not belong to the very thing that life is, and in so far as it is life at all, to the highest source and principle of life: that we can confess nothing but the highest and only true God. Therefore, those souls which are called by the Manichaeans evil, either lack life, and are not souls, neither want nor want anything, desire or flee; or if they lived, so that they could be souls, and do something such as they think, they could not live in any way but life; We would admit that there is no reason why all souls, since souls cannot exist except by living, were created and sustained by Christ, that is, by life.

If the light which is perceived by the sense has God as its author, as the Manichaeans admit, much more the soul which is perceived by the intellect alone.

2. But if at that time my thought could not bear and sustain the question of life itself and of the participation of life; which is certainly great, and in need of

much serene discussion among the most learned; Perhaps I should have been able to discern that which is very evident to every man who considers himself without the study of the parts, that all that we are said to know and to know is grasped either by the sense of the body or by the intelligence. And the senses of the body are generally numbered as five, seeing, hearing, smelling, tasting, and touching: in all of which I excel far and wide in intelligence, who would grant me not even an ungrateful and impious one? When this was established and established, I would achieve that, so that everything that could be physically felt by touch and sight, or in any other way, would be so much inferior to what we would achieve by understanding, inasmuch as we would see the senses themselves yield to intelligence. Wherefore since all life, and for this reason every soul, can be perceived by no bodily sense, but by the intellect alone; but this sun and the moon and all the light which is seen by these mortal eyes are said by the Manichaeans themselves to be ascribed to the true and good God: to preach that it belongs to God, which we look through the body, is utter madness. that we should take it not only with the mind, but with the very sublimity of the soul, that is, with the mind and intelligence, that is to say, to think that life, whatever it may be called, nevertheless life, to be deprived and widowed by the same God. For what is it to live, and how secret from all bodily sense, and how completely incorporeal, if I were to ask God myself, I should not be able to answer? Or should they not also admit that they not only live those souls which they detest, but also live immortally? And what was said by Christ: Let the dead bury their dead 2; It was not said of those who do not live at all, but of those who sin, which is the only death of the immortal soul. Paul writing: The widow that lives in pleasures is dead, 3 for at the same time he said she was dead and alive. Wherefore I would not pay attention to how much more discolored a sinful soul lives, but only to the fact that it lives. If I could not perceive except by understanding, I believe it would occur to me that every soul of light which we perceive through these eyes is to be preferred, as much as we would prefer intelligence to the eyes themselves.

The whole body is also proved to be from God. That soul which is called evil by the Manichaeans, is better in the light.

But they also confirm that this light is from the Father of Christ: should I not doubt that every soul is from him? But I, not only about the soul, but also about any body, if it was not from him, I would not know anything at all, not even then, that is, a man of that inexperience and of that age, if the form was what it was or what was formed, what appearance and what was clothed in appearance, then what I would think piously and cautiously what the cause of these was.

3. But in the meantime I am silent about the body: I complain about the soul, about spontaneous and lively movement, about action, about life, about immortality: in short, I complain that I most pitifully believed that all these things could have anything without the goodness of God; I was carelessly attentive to how great they were; I think that this should make me groan, that I should sigh. I would take these things with me, I would talk with myself, I would convey them to them: I would propose what was the power of understanding how there was nothing in man that we could contribute to this excellence. Where men, if only they were men, would have granted me this; I would like to ask whether to see with these eyes, that is to understand. When they had denied it, I would have concluded that the intelligence of the mind is far from being preferred to the sense of the eyes; then I would add that what we perceive better in reality must necessarily be judged better. Who would not give this? Therefore, I would continue to inquire whether that soul, which they said was evil, was felt by these eyes, or was it understood by the mind? They would admit it mentally. With all of them agreeing and being established among us, I would show what was to be done; That is to say, that soul which they cursed, that light which they venerated was better: since the latter is known by the understanding of the mind, the latter by the sense of the body. Here, however, they would perhaps stick, and refuse to follow the leader's reason: such is the power of old-fashioned opinions and long defended and believed falsity. But I would insist that they adhere more, not harshly, not childishly, not stubbornly; I would repeat what has been granted; and I would show how they were to be granted. I exhorted them to consult in common, that they might certainly see what was to be denied to us; whether the understanding should be preferred to these carnal lights, or whether they would think it false that the excellence of the soul is more excellent than what is known by the vile sense of the body; whether the sun and the moon would not be recognized except by these eyes. But if they had observed that none of these things could be denied except in the most absurd and impudent way; I would suggest that it is not necessary for

them to doubt, that this light which they preached to be worshiped, that soul was worthier than that which they warned to flee from.

Even the soul of a fly is superior to that light.

4. And here, if by chance they asked me, disturbed, whether I considered even the soul of a fly to offer itself to this light, I would answer: Yes; nor would a fly frighten me because it is small, but because it would be alive. For the question is, what causes those limbs to grow so small, what causes a small body to move hither and thither by natural appetite, what moves the feet of a runner in number, what controls and vibrates the feathers of a flyer. Whatever it is, to those who consider it well, it stands out so great in such a small thing, that it is preferable to any glare that dazzles the eyes.

Vicious souls, though damnable, how can they set before this light, which is to be praised in its kind.

Certainly, what no one doubts, whatever it is, is intelligible: that it is superior to all sensible, and for this reason even to this light, divine laws. For what we perceive by thought, please, if we do not perceive this, it is one thing to understand with the mind, another thing to feel through the body, and first to separate the former from the latter by an incomparable sublimity; and therefore cannot the intelligible be preferred to the sensible, since the intellect itself is preferred only to the senses?

5. From this I would perhaps also know it; which is evidently consequent, when injustice and intemperance, and the rest of the vices of the mind, are not felt, but understood; how is it that even those things which we detest and consider to be condemned, yet since they are intelligible, come before this light, when in their kind they are to be praised. For it is suggested to the mind that submits itself well to God, first of all, not everything that we praise, everything that we blame, should be preferred. Nor, because I praise the purest lead, do I esteem it more highly than gold, by reproaching it for this reason. For there is something to be considered in its own kind. I do not trust a lawyer who is ignorant of

many laws: but I prefer him to the most approved tailor, so much so that I do not even think he can be compared. But I praise him because he is the most skilled in his art; but I rightly criticize him because he fulfills his profession less. From which I should find that this light, which was perfect in its own kind, is rightly to be praised: nevertheless, since it is included in the number of sensible things, which the kind of intelligibles must yield to the kind, unjust and intemperate souls must be deputed below, since they are intelligible, although we do not judge these as worthy of wrongful condemnation. For we seek in these things that God may be won over, not that these things should be preferred to the glory. Therefore, I would not oppose anyone who contends that this light is from God; but rather I would say that souls, even vicious ones, not in so far as they are vicious, but in so far as they are souls, must confess that God is their creator.

Or even the faults themselves, as intelligible, are to be preferred to sensible light, and to be attributed to God as the author.

6. If at this point any one of them, cautious and watchful, now even more studious than persistent, should remind me, that we should not look for vicious minds, but for the vices themselves; if they are superior to all sensible things, why should it be agreed among us that light should be attributed to God as the author, but no one but a blasphemer would say that God is the author of vices? of which, if I had deserved and been able to do neither, I would have postponed the commencement; and I confess that it was difficult and arduous to discern what the purpose was. I would return to myself, prostrate myself to God, and groan deeply, seeking that he would not suffer me to be stuck in the middle space, in which I had advanced by certain reasons; lest by a dangerous question I should be compelled either to submit and subdue intelligible things to the sensible, or to call him the author of vices; since both of these were the most full of falsehood and impiety. In no way could I imagine that he would leave me feeling like that. He would rather remind me in those ineffable ways of his, that I should consider again and again whether the vices of the mind, about which I was raging, were to be numbered among the intelligible. That I might find, on account of the infirmity of my inner eye, which had rightly befallen me by my sins, that I might contrive a step for me to grasp the invisible things in the visible ones: of which we would by no means have a more certain knowledge,

but a more reliable practice. And so, I would at once inquire what properly pertains to the sense of the eyes: I would find the colors of which that light should obtain the preeminence. For these are things which no other sense reaches: for the motions of bodies, and sizes, and distances, and shapes, although they can be perceived by the eyes, not properly, but also by the touch. From this I would conclude that the light afforded to the rest of the corporeal and sensible things was as much brighter as the sight was to the other senses. I chose, then, from all that is felt by the body, that light in which I strived, and in which I would necessarily place that stage of my inquiry; I would continue to pay attention to what was going on in this way, and I would talk to myself in this way: If this sun, visible with such clarity and sufficient for the light of the day, should gradually fail in our sight until the likeness of the moon, would we perceive anything else with our eyes but the light shining in any way? yet seeking the light, not seeing what had been, and absorbing it by seeing what was present? Therefore, we would not see that failure, but the light which remained in the failure. But when we did not see, we would not feel; for whatever we perceive by sight cannot be unseen: wherefore, if that defect were not felt either by sight or by any other sense, it could not be numbered among the sensibles. For there is nothing sensible that cannot be felt. Let us now turn our consideration to virtue, by the intelligible light of which we most appropriately say that the mind shines. Moreover, from this light a certain lack of virtue, not destroying the soul, but darkening it, is called a vice. Therefore the defect of the soul can rightly be numbered among the intelligibles, just as that lack of light is rightly excluded from the number of sensibles: yet that which remains of the soul, that is, that which lives and is the soul itself, is just as intelligible as that which is sensible which is in this visible light after failure, however much it shines: and therefore the soul, insofar as it is a soul, and participates in life, without which there can be no soul at all, is most rightly put before all sensible things. Wherefore it is a great error to say that any soul is not of God, from whom you boast that the sun and the moon are.

If visible light is from God, much more from him is the soul, which in so far as it lives is an intelligible thing, even if it is defective.

7. Now if it pleases me to name all sensible things, not only those which we feel, but also those which, not feeling, yet we judge through the body, as through

the eyes of darkness, and through the ears of silence; for we know these things by not seeing them, and this by not hearing them; but even those things which are averted by the privation of enlightenment itself, such as is foolishness, which I should properly call the darkness of the mind: I would make no controversy about the word, but would dissolve the whole question by an easy division, and would at once approve of those who are attentive, that intelligible substances should be preferred to sensible substances by the divine and incorruptible law of truth, not by theirs. lack of substance; although these are intelligible, we would like to call them sensible. Therefore, those who would admit that both these visible lights and those intelligible souls are substances, I compel them in every way to concede and attribute the most sublime parts to souls; But the defects of both kinds cannot be placed one before the other, for they deprive only, and show that they do not exist, that they always have the same force as the negations themselves. For when we say: There is no gold, and: There is no virtue; although there is a great deal between gold and virtue, yet nothing is distant between the negations which we have attached to them. For it is true that it is worse not to have virtue than not to have gold: no sane person wanders from here; Who does not understand that this happens not because of the negations themselves, but because of the things to which they are added? For as much as virtue affords with gold, it is as much more miserable to be without virtue than gold. Wherefore, when intelligible things take precedence over sensible things, we justly tolerate a deficiency in intelligible things more painfully than in sensible things; valuing not the defects of them, but the things that are lacking, more dearly or more cheaply. From which it is already evident that the lack of life, which is intelligible, is much more pitiable than that of this sensible light; because, of course, life understood is much more precious than this light seen.

8. These things being so, will any man dare, when the sun and the moon, and whatever in the stars, in short, whatever shines in this fire of ours and the visible light of the earth, give to God, any souls, which certainly are not souls except by living, since there is only this light life precedes, will you not admit that it is from God? and when he speaks the truth, who says: In so far as it shines, it is from God; Finally, God be great, would I be lying if I said: In so far as he lives, he is from God? Let not, I pray thee, the blindness of the mind and the punishments of the minds increase so much, that men do not understand these

things. But in whatever way their error or obstinacy might have been, I relied on these and armed with reasons, I believe that when I had brought the matter to them so considered and perceptive, and had calmly agreed with them, I was afraid lest any of them should appear to me to be of any importance, if either their understanding, or those things which they understood they would not be perceived through a defect, he would try to prefer it to the sense, or at least to compare it with the corporeal, or with those things which would similarly belong to the same sense of knowing. By what arrangement, when he or anyone should dare to deny to me, that souls, however evil they may be, since they were souls, should be included in the number of intelligible things, and that they should not be intelligible through failure? Indeed, souls would be in no other place than in what they lived. For though they should be understood as defective by deficiency, because they are defective by want of virtue; not, however, through the deficiency of the soul, because the soul is living. Nor is it possible that the presence of life is the cause of failure; when so much and everything fails, as much as it is abandoned by life.

9. In every way, then, since it was evident that no souls could be separated from that author, from whom this light is not separated; Now I would not accept whatever they brought, and I would rather warn them that they should prefer to follow them with me, who preached that everything that was, because it was, in whatever amount it was, was from one God.

The passages of Scripture are objected to by the Manichaeans. How evil is from God, and not from God.

They would recite against me those evangelical voices: That is why you do not hear, because you are not of God; You are of your father the devil. I would also recite on the contrary: All things were made through him, and without him nothing was made; and that of the Apostles: One God from whom all things; and one Lord Jesus Christ through whom all things; and again of the same Apostle: From whom are all things, through whom are all things, in whom are all things, to himself glory 8: and to exhort men (if indeed I could find men), we should not presume to have found anything; but we should rather seek teachers who would show peace and harmony to those opinions which seemed to us to be at war with each other. For in one and the same authority of the Scriptures, when elsewhere it sounded: All things are from God; and elsewhere: You are not of God: since it would be wrong to condemn books at random, who would not see that an expert teacher, who knew the solution of this question, had to be found? who indeed, if he were a good intellectual, and, as it is divinely said, a spiritual man, since he would necessarily favor the true reasons, which I have treated and discussed as far as I could concerning the intelligible and sensible nature, nay, he would himself have opened them much better and more suitable for teaching; We would hear nothing else from him on this question, except how it could be done, so that no race of souls was not from God, and yet it would be rightly said to sinners and unbelievers: You are not from God. For perhaps even we, imploring God for help, could easily see that it is one thing to live and another to sin: and although life in sins is called death in comparison with a righteous life. yet both can be found in one man, so that he is alive and a sinner at the same time: but what is alive is from God; that a sinner, not from God. In which division we use that part of the two which corresponds to our opinion: that when we want to insinuate the omnipotence of God the Creator, we also say to sinners that they are from God. For we call those who are contained in some form, we say animate, we say rational, and lastly, what is most relevant to the matter, we say living: all of these are in themselves divine gifts. But when it is proposed to accuse the wicked, we rightly say: You are not of God. For we say that they are turning away from the truth, unbelievers, criminals, criminals, and, which includes all in one name, sinners: which, again, who doubts that all things are not from God? And so, Christ, rebuking sinners because they were sinners and did not believe in himself, is it any wonder if he says: You are not of God; on the other hand, that sentence remaining intact, that: All things were made through him; and All things from God? For if one does not believe in Christ, rejects Christ's coming, does not receive Christ, it would be a sure sign of souls that are not of God; and therefore it would have been said: You do not hear because you are not of God: how could that word of the Apostle be true, in the very memorable beginning of the Gospel, in which it is said: He came on his own, and his own did not receive him? Wherefore are they theirs, if they have not received it: or whence therefore they are not theirs, because they have not received it: except because men are sinners, in that they are men, to God, because sinners belong to the devil? Here, therefore, he held part of the nature which says: They did not receive him; but he of the will, who says: You are not of God. For the evangelist commended the works of God, Christ checked the sins of men.

They ask where evil comes from, and the Manichaeans think that they can overcome this question. Let them first know that it is very easy, that nothing can live without God. The highest evil is not known except by knowing the highest good, which is God.

10. Perhaps someone will say at this point: Whence sins themselves, and whence evil at all? If from man, whence man? If from an angel, where did the angel come from? When it is said that they are from God, although it is said correctly and truly, yet the ignorant and less powerful seem to look keenly at hidden things, as if evils and sins were connected to God by some chain. By this question they think they rule: as if to ask is to know. Would that it were; no one will be found more knowledgeable than me. But I do not know how often, in disputing a great question, the proposer of a great question displays the person of a great teacher, usually the very person whom he frightens, and is more learned in the thing about which he frightens. And so, these consider themselves preferable to the multitude, because they ask the former what they do not know with the multitude. But if, at the time when I was with them, and not as I have been for a long time now, he repented of having acted, if they had objected to me with these reasons of displeasure, I would say: Please, in the meantime, understand with me that it is very easy, if nothing can shine without God, much less can anything live without God; lest we remain in such monstrous opinions, that I do not know which souls we predict to have life without God. For in this way it may perhaps happen that what you do not know with me, that is, whence the evil is, we shall learn at some time, either together, or in any order. What if the knowledge of the highest evil cannot happen to man without the knowledge of the highest good? For we would not know darkness if we were always in darkness: but knowledge of light does not allow its opposite to be unknown. Now that is the highest good, above which nothing can be: but God is good, and nothing can be higher than God: therefore, God is the highest good. Let us therefore know God, and thus that which we seek first will not be hidden from us. Do you think that the average business is finally or meritorious to the knowledge of God? For what other reward is promised to us than eternal life, which is the knowledge of God? For

the Master God said: This is eternal life, that they may know you, the only and true God, and Jesus Christ, whom you sent. when he turns to God, the merit of attaining eternal life is eternal life, as has been said, knowledge itself. But no one can turn to God unless he turns away from this world. I find this very hard and difficult for me: if it is easy for you, God himself will see. I would like to believe, if it did not move me, that since this world, from which we are commanded to turn away, is visible, and the Apostle said: The things that are seen are temporal; but those things which are not seen are eternal: you are given more to the judgment of these eyes than of the mind, among whom it is preached and believed that there is no shining feather that does not shine from God, and that there is a living soul that does not live from God. These and similar things I would either say to them or consider them with myself. For I could, as it is said, imploring God with all my bowels, and paying as much attention to the Scriptures as was permitted, even then perhaps I might either say such things, or think what was sufficient for salvation.

Augustine was deceived by his familiarity with the Manichaeans and by the success of the victory he had won over the ignorant Christians. The Manichaeans, too, from the knowledge of sin and of the will, are easily reproved.

11. But two things especially, which easily take hold of that unwary age, by admirable circumambulation; whose familiarity is one, I do not know how creeping in a kind of image of goodness, like some winding chain wrapped around the neck in many ways. Another thing is that a certain injurious victory has almost always resulted for me in debates with those who argue with ignorant Christians, but who nevertheless strive to defend their faith competitively, as each one could. With this success, the youth's courage slipped too often, and by his impetuousness he inadvertently verged on a great evil. The kind of quarreling that I had begun after hearing them, whatever I could by my own wit or by any other lessons, I most willingly gave to them alone. Thus, from their words, the ardor of their struggles, from the results of their struggles, love was renewed in them every day. From that time, he approached that whatever they said, about some strange diseases, not because I knew, but because I wished it to be true, I approved it as true. So it happened that,

although slowly and cautiously, I followed men for a long time, preferring the shiny stubble to the living soul.

12. Be true, I could not at that time judge and distinguish the sensible from the intelligible, that is, the carnal from the spiritual; He was not of age, not of discipline, not even of any custom, and not of any merit; for it is not a matter of small joy and happiness: could I not even grasp that which, in the judgment of all men, by the laws of the most high God, nature itself has established?

Sin is committed only by the will. His life and will are known to everyone. The will is what it is.

For any men, whom no folly had broken off from the common sense of the human race, which would have led them to judge studies, whatever inexperience, whatever slowness; I would like to find out what they would answer to my question, whether it seemed to them that they had sinned, because someone else had written something scandalous about the sleeping person's hand. Who doubts that it was so? From whom I would, by whatever means I could, be reconciled and restored to counsel, so that they would not trouble me with asking another thing so manifest, and placed in the knowledge of all. If someone stronger had done something similarly evil, whether because he knew it, although he did not want it at all, would he be held to be guilty of any sin? And here they all wondered at me that I had made such a decision, without hesitation they answered that there was nothing wrong with this at all. Why so? Because anyone who has done something wrong without being aware of it, or not being able to resist, cannot be justly condemned in any way. And the same reason why it was so, if I inquired into the human nature itself in those men, I could easily arrive at what I desired, by asking in this way: What if, while sleeping, he already knew what another was going to do with his hand, and on purpose, he drank more so that he would not wake up , he would give himself up to sleep, in order to deceive someone by swearing; would any sleep give him any evidence of innocence? What else would they pronounce but a guilty man? But if he also willingly was bound, so as to deceive someone with a similar pretense of defense, what did those bonds profit him in the end, that he might be free from sin? Although bound by these, he would not really be able to resist; as he was asleep, completely unaware of what would happen next. Is it then to be doubted that both were judged to have sinned? With these concessions, I would conclude that there is no sin except in the will: since it would also help me that justice holds sinners by their evil will alone, although they have not been able to fulfill what they wanted.

13. Could anyone who deals with these things say that I am engaged in dark and hidden things, where, because of the fewness of those who understand, the suspicion of fraud or ostentation is usually born? Let that distinction between the intelligible and the sensible cease for a while: let me not be envied, because I pursue slow souls with the spurs of subtle discussions. Let me know that I live, let me know that I will to live: in which, if the human race consents, our will is as well known to us as our life. And when we profess this knowledge, we must fear lest anyone should convince us that it is possible to be deceived: for this very thing no one can be deceived, if he either does not live, or does not wish to do anything. I do not think that I have introduced anything obscure, and I am afraid that I should appear to be blamed to no one else, because these things are too obvious: but let us consider what these things mean.

What is the will?

14. Therefore one does not sin except by will. But our will is very well known to us: for I would not know that I will, if I did not know what the will itself is. It is therefore defined in this way: Will is the emotion of the mind, under no compulsion, to either not lose something, or to gain it. Why, then, could I not define it like that? Or was it difficult to see that the unwilling is the opposite of the willing, so that we say that the opposite of the left is the right, and not as black and white? For the same thing cannot be both black and white at the same time. At the same time, indeed, both are one man, but at the same time both are in no way related to one man. Thus, unwillingly and willingly, one mind can be at the same time; but it is impossible to will one and the same thing at the same time. For when every one does something unwillingly, if you ask him whether he wants to do it, he says that he will not: likewise, if you ask him whether he wants not to do it, he answers that he will. Thus you will find the unwilling to do, but the willing not to do: for that is one mind having both at

the same time, but referring one thing to another. Why do I say these things? Because if we ask again why he does it unwillingly, he will say that he was forced. For every one doing it unwillingly is compelled; and every one who is compelled, if he does, does so only unwillingly. It remains that the willing is free from coercion, even if anyone thinks he is under coercion. And in this way everyone who willingly does it is not forced; and everyone who is not compelled either does willingly or does not. When nature itself proclaims these things in all men, whom we can not absurdly question, from the child to the old man, from the schoolboy to the only sage; Why did I not then see that in the definition of the will it should be put: No coercion, which I now put as the most cautious as a result of greater experience? But if this is manifest everywhere, and not by doctrine, but by nature readily available to all; What remains that seems obscure, unless perhaps there is something hidden, that we want something when we want it, and that our mind is moved to it, and that we either have it or do not have it, and if we have it we want to keep it, if we don't have it we want to acquire it? Wherefore every one who wills wants either not to lose, or to gain something. Wherefore, if all these things are clearer in the light, as they are, and not mine only, but the knowledge of the human race given by the liberality of the truth itself, why could I not say at that time also: The will is the movement of the soul, under no compulsion, to either not lose something, or to gain it?

What is a sin?

15. Someone will say: And what would this help you against the Manichaeans? Wait; without first also defining sin, which cannot exist without the will, every mind reads with itself what is divinely written. Therefore sin is the will to retain or achieve what justice forbids, and from which one is free to abstain. However, if there is no freedom, there is no will. But I preferred to define it more roughly than more scrupulously. Were these dark books for me to search, so that I might learn that no one is worthy of reproach or punishment, who either wills what justice does not forbid, or does not do what he cannot do? Do not the shepherds in the mountains, and the poets in the theaters, and the uneducated in the circles, and the learned in the libraries, and the teachers in the schools, and the ancients in the sacred places, and the human race all over the world sing these things? But if no one is worthy of reproach or condemnation, either not

doing contrary to the prohibition of justice, or not doing what he cannot do, every sin is either to be reproached or to be condemned; Who can then doubt that it is a sin, since it is both unjust to will and free not to will? and therefore that definition is both true and the easiest to understand, and not only now, but also then it could have been said by me: Sin is the will to retain or obtain what justice forbids, and whence is it free to abstain?

From the given definitions of sin and the will, he overthrows the whole heresy of the Manichaeans.

16. Come now, let us see what these things will help us. So much so that I desired nothing more: for they would end the whole cause. For whoever, having thoroughly penetrated the secrets of his conscience and the divine laws of nature, consulting with his inner mind, where they are more expressive and certain, admits that these two definitions of will and sin are true, he condemns the whole heresy of the Manichaeans in the fewest and briefest, but clearly most invincible arguments, without any hesitation. That can be considered as such. They say that there are two kinds of souls, one good, which is from God in such a way that it is not made from any matter or nothing from him, but is said to have proceeded from his very substance in some part; they believe and recommend to be believed: and therefore they preach that the former is the highest good, and the latter the highest evil: and that these two kinds were once distinct, but are now mixed. I had not yet heard of the nature and cause of this mixture, but I could now inquire whether that evil race of souls, before it was mixed with good, had any will. For if he had not, he was without sin and innocent, and therefore in no way evil. And if, therefore, evil, because it may exist without will, like fire, yet if it touches good, violates and corrupts it: how much evil is it, and the nature of evil, to be so strong as to change any part of God, and to believe that the supreme good is corruptible and corruptible? But if the will was inherent, surely there was inherent, without any coercion, the emotion of the mind either not to lose something, or to gain it. Now this something was either good, or was thought to be good: for it could not be desired otherwise. But in extreme evil, before the mixture which they preach, there never was any good. Where, then, could there be either knowledge or good opinion? Did they not want anything that was with them, and did they desire that good and truth that was outside? But this will is excellent and to be

preached with great praise, by which the highest and true good is desired. Whence, then, in the most evil emotion of the mind, are we worthy of so much praise? Or did they desire to do harm? First, the system revolves in the same way. For he who wishes to harm, wishes to deprive another of some good for the sake of some good of his own. There was, then, in them either the knowledge of good, or the opinion, which should in no way be of the highest evil. Then, when that good was placed outside themselves, to whom they sought to harm, whether it existed at all, how did they know it? If they had understood, what could be more excellent in such a mind? Or is there anything else, by which all good things are sought with great labors, except that this supreme and sincere good may be understood? What, therefore, is now granted to a few good and just people, but then that mere evil could no longer be helped by any good? But if those souls wore bodies, and had seen it with their eyes; What tongues, what breasts, what talents are sufficient to praise and preach with these eyes, with which the minds of the just can scarcely be equaled? How much good we find at the top of evil! For if it is bad to see God, God is not good: but God is good: therefore, it is good to see God; and I do not know what can be compared to this good. Moreover, since seeing is good, how can it be that being able to see is bad? Therefore, whatever he did either in those eyes or in those minds, so that the divine substance could be seen by them, he did a great and ineffable good worthy of praise. But if it was not done, but was itself such and eternal in itself, it is difficult to find anything better than this evil.

It follows from the just condemnation of evil souls that they are evil, not by nature, but by will.

17. Finally, in order that those souls who are forced to have these reasons have nothing to praise them, I would ask whether God condemns some or no souls. If there are none, there is no judgment of merits, no providence, and the world is governed by chance rather than by reason, or rather is not governed: for administration is not to be given to chance. Now if this is wrong to believe in all those bound by any religion, it remains that either there is damnation of some souls, or there are no sins. But if there are no sins, there is also no evil. It is therefore agreeable to me with them that some souls are condemned by the divine law and judgment. But if these are good, what is justice? If bad; by

nature, or by will? But they by no means claim that the nature of the soul is evil. Where do we teach this? On the previous definitions of will and sin. Because to say that souls are evil, and to sin nothing, is full of madness; and to hold anyone guilty of sin, because he did not do what he could not do, is the highest iniquity and madness. Wherefore those souls do whatever they do, if they do it by nature and not by will, that is, if they lack the free motion of the soul both to do and not to do; If, in short, no power is granted to them to abstain from their work, we cannot hold their sin. But all admit that both evil souls are justly condemned, and those who have not sinned, are unjustly condemned; therefore, they admit that those who sin are bad. And they, as reason taught, do not sin. Therefore, I do not know the kind of evil souls that is foreign, which is introduced by the Manichaeans, there is none.

That souls are good by nature, to whom forgiveness of sins is given.

18. Now let us see that kind of good, which again they praise in such a way that they say it is the very substance of God. But how much better is it that each one should know his rank and merit, and not fan himself with such sacrilegious pride, that when he feels that he is often changed, he believes that there is substance to that supreme good, which unchangeable pious reason professes and teaches? For behold, since it is manifest that souls do not sin in that they are not such as they cannot be; from which it is now clear that I do not know which of these introductions are in any way sinful, and therefore that they are not at all: it is left, that since they admit that they are sins, they do not find to whom to attribute them, except to the good race of souls and the substance of God. But they are urged most of all by Christian authority: for they never denied that sins should be forgiven, when everyone was converted to God; They never said (like many other things) that any corrupter inserted this into the divine Scriptures. To whom, then, are sins given? If they are alien to those evils, they can also become good, they can inherit the kingdom of God with Christ. This because they deny, and have no other kind, except those which they hold to be of the substance of God; it remains for them to admit that not only they also sin, but they themselves sin. But I do not contend that they should sin alone: nevertheless, they sin. But are they compelled by the combination of evils? If they are compelled in such a way that there is no power to resist, they do not sin: if it is in their power to resist, and they consent of

their own free will, why so many good things in the greatest evil, why this evil in the greatest good, we are forced to find by their teaching; except because it is neither that evil which they induce with suspicion, nor this supreme good which they pervert with superstition?

From the determination of the evil and the good, there are not two kinds of souls. Granted that the species of souls are prone to vice, not to follow them is by nature evil, otherwise it is the highest good.

19. But if I had taught them to be delirious and to err about these two kinds of souls, or at least I had learned them myself, what could remain, why should they now appear to me to be heard or consulted on any matter? Or should I learn from this showing that there are two kinds of souls, that in deliberating, the assent nods now in the direction of evil, now in the direction of good? Why is this not more a sign of one soul, which can be carried hither and thither by its free will, hither and thither? For when it happens to me, I feel that I am one, considering both, choosing one over the other; Nor is it surprising, for we are now constituted in such a way that we can be affected by pleasure through the flesh and honorably through the spirit. Why do I not compel two souls from here to confess? For we can better and much more readily understand the two kinds of good things, neither of which is alien from the author God, affecting one soul from different parts, the lower and the higher, or, as may properly be said, the outer and the inner. These are the two kinds which we treated a little before under the name of sensible and intelligible, which we more willingly and familiarly call carnal and spiritual. But it has become difficult for us to abstain from carnal things, since our truest bread is spiritual. For we now eat bread with labor. For we are not under any penalty for the sin of transgression, mortals from immortals. Therefore, it happens that when those who are trying to do better for us, having become accustomed with our flesh and our sins to make a kind of war against us, and to make it difficult for us, some fools suspect another kind of souls that is not from God in the most obtuse superstition.

20. Although even if it were granted to them that we are guilty of other inferior kinds of souls, they do not thereby conclude either that they are evil by nature, or that these are the highest good. For it is possible that by their own will they

desired what was not lawful, that is, by sinning, evils were made from good; and again they may become good, but as it happens, as long as they remain in sin, they bring other things to themselves by a kind of secret persuasion: then, that they may not be bad at all, but in their kind, though inferior, perform their proper work without any sin. Supreme justice will give the superior ruler of things, if they wish to follow and imitate those inferiors, by sinning they become bad, not because they are bad, but because they are badly imitated. For by them the proper is dealt with, by the latter the foreign is desired: whence the former remain at their own level, the latter sink to the lower, as when men follow beasts. For a four-footed horse walks beautifully: but if this man imitates him with his feet and hands, who will think him worthy of eating even straw? Therefore, we generally condemn the imitator rightly, when we test him whom he imitates. Now we disapprove, not because he did not achieve it, but because he wanted to achieve it at all. For we test that in the horse, to whom we prefer a man, so much so that we are offended by the fact that it is followed by inferiors. What among the people themselves, in sending out the voice that the herald does well, even if the senator does it more clearly and better than the herald, is he mad? Take this matter: the shining moon is praised, and it pleases those who consider well its course and turns; yet if the sun wishes to imitate her (for let us imagine that he can have such wishes), who is not most and rightly displeased? From which it is that I want to be understood. Even if there are souls (which in the meantime is uncertain) given over to corporeal duties, not by sin, but by nature, and although they are inferior, they still touch us in some interior proximity, they should not therefore be considered evil, because we too, when we follow them and love corporeal things, we are bad For this reason we sin by loving the corporeal, because we are commanded and able by nature to love spiritual things and justice, and then we are the best and happiest of our kind.

21. Wherefore, what is the effect of the argument, which is heated in both directions, sometimes prone to sin, sometimes subjugated to right action, so that we are forced to accept that there are two kinds of souls, the nature of one of which is from God, and the other is not, when we conjecture so many other causes of alternating thought may it be allowed? But anyone who is a good thinker of things sees that these things are obscure, and that it is impossible to search for them by sly minds. Wherefore those things which have been said concerning the will and sin, those things, I say, which the highest justice

permits no one who uses reason to be ignorant of, those things which, if they are taken away from us, there is nothing from which to begin the training of virtue, nothing from which to rise from the death of vices, again and again considered quite clearly and clearly convince them that the heresy of the Manichaeans is false.

Again, from the benefit of repentance, it is shown that souls are not evil by nature.

22. This is similar to what I will now say about repentance. For as is agreed among all the sane, and as the Manichaeans themselves not only admit, but also enjoin, it is useful to repent of sin. What am I now to collect in this matter the testimonies of the divine Scriptures, which have been spread far and wide? This is also the voice of nature: the knowledge of this matter has left no one foolish; if this were not deeply ingrained in us, we would perish. A man may say that he has not sinned: but he will not dare to say that if he has sinned, he is not to be repented of. Being so, I ask, of these two classes of souls, which one should repent of sin? I know indeed that it cannot be of him who does evil, nor of him who cannot do good: therefore, to use their words, if the soul of the darkness of sin repents, it is not of the substance of the highest evil; if you light the soul, it is not of the substance of the highest good. For that feeling of repentance, which is profitable, testifies both that the penitent has done evil, and that he could have done good. How, then, can there be no harm from me, if I have done wrong? or how can I rightly repent if I have not done it? Listen to the other part: How can anything good come from me, in whom there is a good will? or how can I rightly repent if it is not present? Wherefore they either deny that there is a great benefit to repentance, so that they are driven not only by the Christian name, but by every imaginary reason; or those two kinds of souls, the one from which there is no evil, the other from which there is no good, let them cease to speak and teach; for if they do, they will certainly cease to be Manichaeans; for the whole of that sect is supported by a variety of two-headed, or rather headless, souls.

23. And indeed it is enough for me to know that the Manichaeans err, that I know that sin must be repented of; and yet if now any of my friends, who still

think they should listen to them, I will compel them by the right of friendship, and say to him: Do you know that it is useful when everyone has sinned? repent? without doubt he will swear that he knows. If then, I make you know that the heresy of the Manichaeans is false, will you desire anymore? What more could he want in this matter? So far so good indeed. But when I begin to show the certain and necessary reasons which result in that proposition, as it is said, connected with chains of diamonds, I will bring the whole matter to the conclusion by which it is overthrown. He will perhaps deny that he knows that advantage of repentance, which no learned man, no unlearned man, is ignorant of. and, rather, he strives to know that, when we are in doubt and deliberation, two souls in us apply their proper defenses to each part of the question. O habit of sin! oh count the punishment of sin! You then turned me away from the consideration of such obvious things; but you harmed him who did not feel; but now, in the same way, among my closest relatives who do not feel, I already feel wounded and tormented.

He prays for his friends who have been partners in error.

24. I beseech you, dear ones, attend to these things: I know your talents well. If you now allow me the mind and reason of any man, they are much more certain than what we either seemed to learn there, or rather were compelled to believe. Great God, almighty God, God of the highest goodness, how inviolable and unchangeable it is right to believe and understand, the Triune unity which the Catholic Church worships, I beseech you, experiencing your mercy in me, that men with whom I have been in complete agreement since childhood in every conviction, you are allowed to disagree with me in your worship. I see that it is most expected at this point, how I would even then defend the Catholic Scriptures accused by the Manichees, if, as I say, I were cautious; or now I will show that it can be defended. But in other volumes God will help my purpose; for this already, as far as I think, requires a moderate length of park.

LATIN TEXT

DE DUABUS ANIMABUS

Manichaeorum error de duabus animabus, quarum altera non sit a Deo, qua ratione expugnatur. Anima omnis cum vita quaedam sit, nonnisi a Deo vitae fonte esse potest.

1. Opitulante Dei misericordia, disruptis et derelictis Manichaeorum laqueis, tandem Catholicae gremio restitutum libet considerare nunc saltem ac deplorare illam meam miseriam. Multa enim erant, quae facere debui, ne tam facile ac diebus paucis, religionis verissimae semina mihi a pueritia salubriter insita, errore vel fraude falsorum fallaciumve hominum effossa ex animo pellerentur. Nam primo animarum illa duo genera, quibus ita singulas naturas propriasque tribuerunt, ut alterum de ipsa Dei esse substantia, alterius vero Deum nec conditorem quidem velint accipi, si mecum sobrie diligenterque considerassem, mente in Deum supplici et pia; fortasse mihi satagenti apparuisset, nullam esse qualemlibet vitam, quae non eo ipso quo vita est, et in quantum omnino vita est, ad summum vitae fontem principiumque pertineat: quod nihil aliud quam summum et solum verumque Deum possumus confiteri. Quapropter illas animas, quae a Manichaeis vocantur malae, aut carere vita, et animas non esse, neque quidquam velle seu nolle, appetere vel fugere; aut si viverent, ut et animae esse possent, et aliquid tale agere, quale illi opinantur, nullo modo eas nisi vita vivere: ac si Christum dixisse constaret, ut constat: Ego sum vita 1; nihil esse causae cur non omnes animas, cum animae nisi vivendo esse non possint, per Christum, id est, per vitam creatas et conditas fateremur.

Si lux quae sensu percipitur Deum habet auctorem, ut fatentur Manichaei, multo magis anima quae solo intellectu percipitur.

2. Quod si tempore illo quaestionem de ipsa vita et de participatione vitae mea cogitatio ferre ac sustinere non posset; quae profecto magna est, et multum serenae disputationis inter doctissimos indigens; illud dispicere fortasse valuissem, quod omni homini sese sine studio partium bene consideranti manifestissime apparet, omne quod scire et nosse dicimur, aut sensu corporis,

aut intelligentia nos habere comprehensum. Sensus autem corporis etiam vulgo quinque numerari, visum, auditum, odoratum, gustum, atque tactum: quibus omnibus intelligentiam longe alteque praestare et excellere, quis mihi non vel ingratus impiusque concederet? Quo constituto atque firmato, illud consequi, ut cuncta quae tactu et visu, vel quolibet alio modo corporaliter sentirentur, tanto essent inferiora his quae intellegendo assequeremur, quanto ipsos sensus intelligentiae cedere videremus. Quamobrem cum omnis vita, et ob hoc omnis anima nullo corporis sensu, sed solo intellectu percipi queat; sol autem iste atque luna omnisque lux quae mortalibus his oculis cernitur, ab ipsis quoque Manichaeis vero et bono Deo tribuenda esse dicatur: summam esse dementiam id praedicare pertinere ad Deum, quod per corpus intuemur; quod vero non solum animo, sed ipsa sublimitate animi, mente scilicet atque intelligentia caperemus, id est, vitam, qualiscumque illa diceretur, tamen vitam, eodem Deo auctore privandam et viduandam putare. Num enim quid sit vivere, quamque secretum ab omni corporis sensu, quamque omnino incorporeum, si me ipsum invocato Deo interrogarem, respondere non possim? Aut non illi quoque fateantur, non solum vivere illas, quas detestantur animas, sed etiam immortaliter vivere? Quodque a Christo dictum est: Dimitte mortuos sepelire mortuos suos 2; non de omnino non viventibus, sed de peccantibus dictum, quae immortalis animae sola mors est; scribente Paulo: Mortua est vidua quae in deliciis vivit 3: simul enim et mortuam esse dixit, et vivere. Quare non ego quanto decoloratius vivat peccatrix anima, sed illud ipsum tantum quod vivat attenderem. Quod si percipere nisi intellegendo non possem, credo veniret in mentem, tanto esse quamlibet animam luci, quam per hos sentimus, oculos, praeferendam, quanto intelligentiam ipsis oculis praeferremus.

Corpus etiam omne a Deo esse unde probatur. Animam illam quae mala dicitur a Manichaeis, luce esse meliorem.

Lucem autem illam illi quoque a Patre Christi esse confirmant: egone tandem, quod ab eo esset quaecumque anima, dubitarem? Ego vero non modo de anima, sed de quovis etiam corpore, quin ab ipso esset, nihil omnino, ne tum quidem, homo scilicet illius imperitiae atque illius aetatis ambigerem, si forma quid esset quidve formatum, quid species et quid indutum specie, deinde quid horum cui causa esset, pie cauteque cogitarem.

3. Sed de corpore interim taceo: de anima conqueror, de spontaneo et vivido motu, de actu, de vita, de immortalitate: denique conqueror, quod aliquam rem ista omnia sine Dei bonitate habere posse miserrimus credidi; quod quanta essent, negligenter attendi; hoc mihi gemendum, hoc deflendum puto. Volverem mecum haec, loquerer mecum, deferrem ad illos : quae vis esset intellegendi, quam nihil esset in homine, quod huic excellentiae possemus conferre, proponerem. Ubi mihi hoc homines, si modo essent homines, concessissent; quaererem utrum his oculis videre, id est intellegere. Ubi negavissent, colligerem primo longe esse sensui oculorum istorum intelligentiam mentis anteponendam: deinde subiungerem, id quod re meliore perciperemus, necessario melius iudicandum. Quis hoc non daret? Ergo pergerem quaerere, anima illa, quam malam dicerent, oculisne sentiretur istis, an mente intellegeretur? Mente faterentur. Quibus omnibus inter nos convenientibus atque firmatis, quid conficeretur ostenderem; animam scilicet illam quam exsecrarentur, luce ista quam venerarentur esse meliorem: quandoquidem illa intellectu mentis, haec sensu corporis innotescit. Hic vero haererent fortasse, ducemque rationem sequi recusarent: tanta est vis veternosarum opinionum et diu defensae atque creditae falsitatis. Sed ego instarem magis haerentibus, non aspere, non pueriliter, non pervicaciter; repeterem quae concessa sunt; et quam essent concedenda, monstrarem. Hortarer ut in commune consulerent, viderent certe quid nobis negandum esset; utrum intellectum istis carneis luminibus praeferendum, an excellentius esse quod animi excellentia, quam quod vili sensu corporis cognoscitur, falsum putarent: an illas animas, quas alienigenas crederent, tantum intellegendo, id est, ipsa animi excellentia sciri posse nollent fateri; an solem ac lunam non nisi istis oculis notos fieri vellent abnuere. Quod si nihil horum nisi absurdissime atque impudentissime negari posse animadverterent; suaderem non eos oportere dubitare, istam lucem quam colendam praedicarent, esse anima illa viliorem quam fugiendam monerent.

Anima etiam muscae praestantior ista luce.

4. Atque hic si forte turbati a me quaererent, num etiam muscae animam huic luci praestare censerem: responderem: Etiam; nec me terreret musca quod parva est, sed quod viva firmaret. Quaeritur enim, quid illa membra tam exigua vegetet, quid huc atque illuc pro naturali appetitu tantillum corpusculum

ducat, quid currentis pedes in numerum moveat, quid volantis pennulas moderetur ac vibret. Quod qualecumque est, bene considerantibus, in tam parvo tam magnum eminet, ut cuivis fulgori perstringenti oculos praeferatur.

Vitiosae animae quamquam damnandae, quomodo huic luci, quae in genere suo laudanda est, antecellant.

Certe quod nemo dubitat, quidquid est, intellegibile est: quod omni sensibili, et ob hoc huic etiam luci divinis legibus antecellit. Quid enim cogitatione percipimus, quaeso, si hoc non percipimus, aliud esse mente intellegere, aliud sentire per corpus, et prius illud ab hoc posteriore incomparabili sublimitate distare; ideoque non posse intellegibilia sensibilibus non praeferri, cum ipse intellectus tantum sensibus praeferatur?

5. Hinc illud etiam fortasse cognoscerem; quod consequens esse manifestum est, cum iniustitia et intemperantia caeteraque animi vitia non sentiantur, sed intellegantur; quomodo fiat ut etiam ista, quae detestamur et damnanda censemus, tamen quoniam intellegibilia sunt, anteire hanc lucem queant, cum in suo genere ista laudanda sit. Suggeritur enim animo bene sese Deo subiicienti, primo non omne quod laudamus, omni quod vituperamus, esse anteponendum. Neque enim quia laudo purgatissimum plumbum, ob hoc illud vituperando auro pluris aestimo. In suo enim genere quidque considerandum est. Improbo iurisconsultum multas leges ignorantem: sed eum tamen probatissimo sutori sic praefero, ut ne comparandum quidem putem. At istum laudo, quod suae artis peritissimus sit: illum autem, quod suam professionem minus impleat, iure reprehendo. Ex quo reperire deberem, lucem istam, quod in genere proprio perfecta esset, iure laudari: tamen quia sensibilium rerum numero includitur, quod genus intellegibilium generi cedat necesse est, infra iniustas et intemperantes animas, quoniam sunt intellegibiles, esse deputandam; quamvis istas non iniuria damnatione dignissimas iudicemus. Quaerimus namque in his quod concilietur Deo, non quod isti fulgori praeferatur. Quapropter, quisquis hoc lumen ex Deo esse contenderet, non repugnarem; sed magis animas dicerem, vitiosas etiam, non in quantum vitiosae, sed in quantum animae sunt, Deum sibi esse creatorem fateri oportere.

An ipsa etiam vitia tamquam intelligibilia, luci sensibili praeferenda sint, et Deo ut auctori tribuenda.

6. Hoc loco si quisquam illorum cautus et vigilans, iam etiam studiosior quam pertinacior, me admoneret, non de vitiosis animis, sed de ipsis vitiis esse quaerendum: quae quoniam sensu corporis non cognoscerentur, et tamen cognoscerentur, non nisi intelligibilia posse accipi, quae si sensibilibus omnibus antecellunt, cur lucem Deo auctori esse tribuendam inter nos conveniret, vitiorum vero auctorem Deum nemo nisi sacrilegus diceret: responderem homini, si aut statim et repente, ut bonis Dei cultoribus solet, divinitus infulsisset huius solutio quaestionis, aut fuisset antea praeparata: quorum si neutrum meruissem atque potuissem, coepta differrem; quodque esset propositum, difficile esse ad dignoscendum atque arduum confiterer. Recurrerem in me, prosternerer Deo, alte ingemiscerem, quaerens ne me in medio spatio, quo certis rationibus promovissem, haerere pateretur; ne ancipiti quaestione cogerer aut intellegibilia sensibilibus submittere ac subdere, aut ipsum vitiorum dicere auctorem; cum esset utrumvis horum falsitatis impietatisque plenissimum. Nullo modo possem existimare, quod me sic affectum ille desereret. Admoneret potius suis illis ineffabilibus modis, ut considerarem etiam atque etiam, utrum animi vitia, de quibus aestuarem, inter intellegibilia numeranda essent. Quod ut reperirem, propter imbecillitatem interioris oculi mei, quae mihi peccatis meis iure accidisset, aliquem mihi ad invisibilia contuenda in ipsis visibilibus machinarer gradum: quorum esset nobis nullo modo certior cognitio, sed consuetudo fidentior. Itaque statim quaererem quid ad sensum proprie pertineret oculorum: invenirem colores, quorum principatum lux ista obtineret. Haec enim sunt quae nullus alius sensus attingit: nam motus corporum, et magnitudines, et intervalla, et figuras, quamvis et oculis, non tamen proprie, sed tactu etiam posse sentiri. Unde colligerem tanto caeteris corporeis et sensibilibus praestare lucem, quanto aliis sensibus aspectus esset illustrior. Electa igitur ex omnibus quae corpore sentiuntur ista luce, qua niterer, et in qua gradum illum inquisitionis meae necessario collocarem; pergerem attendere quid ageretur hoc modo, mecumque ita sermocinarer: Si sol iste tanta claritate conspicuus et diei luce sufficiens, usque ad lunae similitudinem in conspectu nostro paulatim deficeret, num aliud quidquam oculis sentiremus quam lucem utcumque fulgentem; lucem tamen quaerentes, quod fuerat non videndo, et haurientes videndo quod

aderat? Non ergo illum defectum videremus, sed lucem quae defectui remaneret. Cum autem non videremus, non sentiremus; quidquid enim sentimus aspectu, non potest non videri: quare, si defectus ille neque visu, neque alio sensu sentiretur, non posset inter sensibilia numerari. Nihil enim sensibile est, quod sentiri non potest. Referamus nunc considerationem ad virtutem, cuius intellegibili luce splendere animum convenientissime dicimus. Porro ab hac luce virtutis defectus quidam non perimens animam, sed obscurans, vitium vocatur. Potest igitur recte vitium quoque animae nequaquam inter intellegibilia numerari, ut lucis ille defectus recte de sensibilium numero eximitur: illud tamen quod remanet animae, id est, hoc ipsum quod vivit atque anima est, tam est intellegibile, quam sensibile illud quod in hoc visibili lumine post defectum quantumcumque fulgeret: et ideo animam in quantum anima esset, et vitae participaret, sine qua nullo pacto anima esse potest, rectissime omnibus sensibilibus anteferri. Quamobrem maximi erroris esse, ullam animam dicere non esse ex Deo, ex quo esse solem lunamque glorieris.

Si lumen visibile a Deo est, multo magis ab ipso anima, quae in quantum vivit intellegibilis res est, etiamsi vitiosa.

7. Quod si iam placeret omnia sensibilia nominare non modo ea quae sentiremus, sed etiam ea quae non sentiendo tamen per corpus iudicaremus, sicut per oculos tenebras, et per aures silentium; et illas enim non videndo, et hoc non audiendo cognoscimus: rursusque intellegibilia, non ea tantum quae illustrata mente conspicimus, sicuti est ipsa sapientia; sed etiam illa quae ipsius illustrationis privatione aversamur, ut est insipientia, quam tenebras animi congrue dixerim: nullam de verbo facerem controversiam, sed totam quaestionem facili divisione dissolverem, statimque approbarem bene attendentibus, substantias intellegibiles sensibilibus substantiis divina et incorrupta veritatis lege praeponi, non earum substantiarum defectus; quamvis hos intellegibiles, illos sensibiles appellare vellemus. Quapropter, qui et haec lumina visibilia, et illas intellegibiles animas substantias esse faterentur, omni modo eos cogi sublimiores partes animis concedere, atque tribuere; defectus vero utriusque generis non posse alteros alteris anteponi, privant enim tantum, et non esse indicant, quod usquequaque eamdem vim habent, sicut ipsae negationes. Nam cum dicimus: Non est aurum, et: Non est virtus; quamvis

inter aurum et virtutem plurimum, nihil tamen inter negationes, quas eis adiunximus, distat. Verum enim vero peius est non esse virtutem, quam non esse aurum: nemo sanus hinc ambigit; quod non propter ipsas negationes, sed propter res quibus adiungantur, accidere quis non intellegat? Auro enim virtus quanto praestat, tanto est virtute quam auro carere miserius. Quamobrem, cum res intellegibiles sensibilibus rebus antecellunt, defectum in intellegibilibus quam in sensibilibus merito aegrius toleramus; non eos defectus, sed ea quae deficiunt, carius vel vilius aestimantes. Ex quo iam illud apparet, defectum vitae, quae intellegibilis est, multo miserabiliorem esse, quam huius sensibilis lucis; quod scilicet multo est carior intellecta vita, quam lux ista conspecta.

8. Quae cum ita sint, audebitne quisquam, cum solem ac lunam, et quidquid in sideribus, quidquid denique in hoc igne nostro atque terreno luce visibili effulget, Deo tribuat, animas quaslibet, quae profecto nisi vivendo animae non sunt, cum tantum hoc lumen vita praecedat nolle concedere ex Deo esse? et cum ille verum dicat, qui dicit: In quantum nitet, ex Deo est; egone tandem, Deus magne, mentiar, si dicam: In quantum vivit, ex Deo est? Non usque adeo, quaeso, caecitas mentis suppliciaque augeantur animorum, ut haec homines non intellegant. Sed quoquo modo illorum error aut pertinacia sese haberet, his ego fretus armatusque rationibus, credo cum ad eos rem ita consideratam perspectamque detulissem, et cum his placide contulissem, vererer ne mihi quisquam eorum alicuius momenti esse videretur, si aut intellectum, aut ea quae intellectu non per defectum perciperentur, sensui conaretur praeferre, aut saltem comparare corporeo, vel his rebus quae ad eumdem sensum cognoscendae similiter pertinerent. Quo constituto, quando ille mihi vel quisquam negare auderet, animas quantum vellet malas, tamen quoniam animae essent, intellegibilium rerum numero contineri, neque illas per defectum intellegi? Siquidem animae non alio essent, nisi quo viverent. Licet enim per defectum intellegerentur vitiosae, quia virtutis egestate vitiosae; non tamen per defectum animae, quia vivendo animae. Nec fieri potest ut vitae praesentia sit causa deficiendi; cum tanto quidque deficiat, quanto deseritur a vita.

9. Omni modo igitur cum pateret non posse ullas animas ab eo auctore separari, a quo lux ista non separatur; iam quidquid afferrent, non acciperem:

moneremque potius, ut eos mecum sequi mallent, qui omne quidquid esset, quoniam esset, in quantumcumque esset, ex uno Deo esse praedicarent.

Obiectantur contra a Manichaeis loca Scripturae. Mali quomodo ex Deo, et non ex Deo.

Recitarent adversus me voces illas evangelicas: Vos propterea non auditis, quia ex Deo non estis 4; Vos ex patre diabolo estis 5. Ego quoque contra recitarem: Omnia per ipsum facta sunt, et sine ipso factum est nihil 6; et illud Apostoli: Unus Deus ex quo omnia; et unus Dominus Iesus Christus per quem omnia 7; et iterum eiusdem Apostoli: Ex quo omnia, per quem omnia, in quo omnia, ipsi gloria 8: hortarerque homines (si tamen homines invenirem), nihil nos iam quasi comperisse praesumeremus; sed quaereremus potius magistros, qui sententiarum istarum, quae nobis inter se pugnare viderentur, pacem concordiamque monstrarent. Nam in una atque eadem auctoritate Scripturarum, cum alibi sonaret: Omnia ex Deo 9; et alibi: Vos non estis ex Deo 10: quoniam Libros temere condemnare nefas esset, quis non videret peritum doctorem, cui quaestionis huius solutio nota esset, inveniendum fuisse? qui profecto si esset bonus intellector, et, ut divinitus dicitur, homo spiritalis 11, quoniam necessario faveret veris rationibus, quas de intellegibili sensibilique natura, quantum potui, tractavi atque disserui, imo eas ipse multo melius, et ad docendum aptius aperiret; nihil ab eo aliud de hac quaestione audiremus, nisi quemadmodum fieri posset, ut et nullum animarum genus non esset ex Deo, et recte tamen peccatoribus et infidelibus diceretur: Non estis ex Deo. Nam et nos fortasse implorato in auxilium Deo facile videre possemus, aliud esse vivere, aliud peccare: et quanquam vita in peccatis in comparatione iustae vitae mors appellata sit 12; utrumque tamen in homine uno posse inveniri, ut simul sit vivus atque peccator: sed quod vivus, ex Deo; quod peccator, non ex Deo. In qua divisione utimur ea parte de duabus, quae nostrae sententiae competit: ut cum Dei conditoris omnipotentiam insinuare volumus, etiam peccatoribus dicamus quod ex Deo sint. Dicimus enim his qui aliqua specie continentur, dicimus animantibus, dicimus rationalibus, dicimus postremo, quod ad rem maxime attinet, viventibus: quae omnia per se ipsa divina sunt munera. Cum autem malos arguere propositum est, recte dicimus: Non estis ex Deo. Dicimus enim se a veritate avertentibus, infidelibus, facinorosis, flagitiosis, et, quod nomine uno totum continet, peccatoribus: quae rursus omnia ex Deo non esse quis dubitet? Itaque Christus peccatoribus, idipsum quod peccatores erant et sibi non credebant coarguens, quid mirum si ait: Non estis ex Deo; ex alia parte illa salva manente sententia quod: Omnia per ipsum facta sunt; et, Omnia ex Deo? Nam si Christo non credere, Christi adventum repudiare, Christum non recipere, certum indicium esset animarum quae non sunt Dei; et ideo dictum esset: Vos propterea non auditis, quia non estis ex Deo: quomodo vera esset vox illa Apostoli, in ipso Evangelii memorabili principio, qua dictum est: In sua propria venit, et sui eum non receperunt 13? Unde sui, si non receperunt: aut unde ideo non sui, quia non receperunt: nisi quia homines peccatores, eo quod sunt homines, ad Deum; eo vero quod peccatores, ad diabolum pertinent? Hic ergo partem naturae tenuit qui ait: Sui eum non receperunt; ille vero voluntatis, qui ait: Non estis ex Deo. Evangelista enim Dei opera commendabat, Christus hominum peccata coercebat.

Quaerunt unde malum, et hac quaestione vincere se putant Manichaei. Cognoscant prius quod facillimum est, nihil vivere posse sine Deo. Summum malum non cognoscitur nisi cognito summo bono, quod est Deus.

10. Hic fortasse quis dicat: Unde ipsa peccata, et omnino unde malum? Si ab homine, unde homo? si ab angelo, unde angelus? Quos ex Deo esse cum dicitur, quamvis recte vereque dicatur, videntur tamen imperitis et minus valentibus acriter res abditas intueri, quasi per quamdam catenam ad Deum mala et peccata connecti. Hac quaestione illi regnare se putant: quasi vero interrogare sit scire. Utinam id esset; nemo me scientior reperiretur. Sed nescio quomodo saepe in altercando magnae quaestionis propositor personam magni doctoris ostentat, plerumque ipse ipso quem terret, in eo de quo terret indoctior. Itaque isti multitudini se praeferendos arbitrantur, quia priores interrogant quod cum multitudine ignorant. Sed si eo tempore quo cum eis me, non sicut iam diu ago, egisse nunc poenitet, mihi has rationes depromenti hoc obiecissent, dicerem: Quaeso, interim cognoscite mecum quod facillimum est, si nihil sine Deo potest fulgere, multo minus posse aliquid vivere sine Deo; ne in tantis monstris opinionum remaneamus, ut nescio quas animas vitam sine Deo habere praedicemus. Sic enim fortasse continget ut id quod mecum ignoratis, id est, unde sit malum, vel simul, vel quolibet ordine aliquando discamus. Quid si enim cognitio summi mali sine cognitione summi boni contingere homini non potest? Non enim nossemus tenebras, si in tenebris

semper essemus: sed lucis notitia contrarium suum non sinit incognitum. Summum autem bonum id est, quo superius esse nihil potest: Deus autem bonum, et Deo superius esse nihil potest : Deus igitur summum bonum. Cognoscamus ergo Deum, atque ita nos illud quod praepropere quaerimus non latebit. Mediocrisne negotii tandem vel meriti cognitionem Dei esse arbitramini? Quod enim nobis aliud praemium, quam vita aeterna promittitur, quae Dei cognitio est? Ait enim magister Deus: Haec est autem vita aeterna, ut cognoscant te solum et verum Deum, et quem misisti Iesum Christum 14. Etenim anima quamvis sit immortalis, tamen quia mors eius recte dicitur a Dei cognitione aversio; cum se convertit ad Deum, meritum est aeternae vitae consequendae, ut sit aeterna vita, sicut dictum est, ipsa cognitio. Converti autem ad Deum nemo, nisi ab hoc mundo se avertat, potest. Hoc ego mihi arduum et difficillimum sentio: vobis si facile est, ille ipse Deus viderit. Ego vellem credere, nisi me moveret, quod cum iste mundus, a quo averti iubemur, visibilis sit, dixitque Apostolus: Ea quae videntur, temporalia sunt; quae autem non videntur, aeterna sunt 15: vos plus istorum oculorum quam mentis iudicio tribuitis, apud quos nullam esse fulgentem pennam quae non ex Deo fulgeat, et esse viventem animam quae non ex Deo vivat, praedicatur et creditur. Haec et his similia vel illis etiam dicerem, vel mecum reputarem. Possem namque Deum omnibus, ut dicitur, visceribus deprecans, et Scripturis quantum licebat intentus, etiam tunc fortasse talia vel dicere, vel quod saluti sat erat cogitare.

Augustinus familiaritate cum Manichaeis et successu victoriae de christianis imperitis a se reportatae deceptus. Manichaei ex cognitione item peccati et voluntatis facile refellendi.

11. Sed me duo quaedam maxime, quae incautam illam aetatem facile capiunt, per admirabiles attrivere circuitus; quorum est unum familiaritas, nescio quomodo repens quadam imagine bonitatis, tamquam sinuosum aliquod vinculum multipliciter collo involutum. Alterum quod quaedam noxia victoria pene mihi semper in disputationibus proveniebat disserenti cum christianis imperitis, sed tamen fidem suam certatim, ut quisque posset, defendere molientibus. Quo successu creberrimo gliscebat adolescentis animositas, et impetu suo in pervicaciae magnum malum imprudenter vergebat. Quod altercandi genus quia post eorum auditionem aggressus eram, quidquid meo vel

qualicumque ingenio vel aliis lectionibus poteram, solis illis libentissime tribuebam. Ita ex illorum sermonibus ardor in certamina, ex certaminum proventu amor in illos quotidie novabatur. Ex quo accedebat ut quidquid dicerent, miris quibusdam morbis, non quia sciebam, sed quia optabam verum esse, pro vero approbarem. Ita factum est ut quamvis pedetentim atque caute, tamen diu sequerer homines nitidam stipulam viventi animae praeferentes.

12. Verum esto, non poteram illo tempore sensibilia ab intellegibilibus, carnalia scilicet ab spiritalibus diiudicare atque discernere; non erat aetatis, non disciplinae, non cuiusdam etiam consuetudinis, non ullorum denique meritorum; non enim parvi gaudii et felicitatis res est: itane tandem ne illud quidem arripere poteram, quod in omnium hominum iudicio summi Dei legibus natura ipsa constituit?

Peccatum nonnisi a voluntate. Vita et voluntas sua cuique notissima. Voluntas quid sit.

Quivis enim homines, quos modo a communi sensu generis humani nulla disrupisset amentia, quae vellent ad iudicandum studia detulissent, quamlibet imperitiam, quantamcumque etiam tarditatem; velim experiri quid mihi responderent roganti, utrum eis peccasse videretur, de cuius dormientis manu scripsisset alius aliquid flagitiosum. Omnes quis dubitet ita fuisse negaturos illud esse peccatum, ita reclamaturos, ut etiam succenserent fortasse quod tali eos rogatione dignos putaverim? A quibus ego, quoquo modo poteram, reconciliatis et in consilium restitutis peterem, ut me aliud tam manifestum, et in omnium cognitione positum, interrogantem non moleste ferrent: tunc quaererem, si non dormientis, sed scientis manu, qui membris tamen caeteris vinctus atque constrictus esset, quisquam valentior aliquid similiter fecisset mali, utrum quia id nosset, quamvis omnino noluisset, ullo peccati nomine teneretur. Et hic mihi omnes mirantes quod talia sciscitarer, sine cunctatione responderent, nihil etiam istum omnino peccasse. Quid ita? Quia de quo nesciente, vel resistere non valente quisquam quidpiam mali fecerit, iuste damnari nullo modo potest. Atque idipsum cur ita esset, si in illis hominibus naturam ipsam percontarer humanam, facile pervenirem ad id quod cuperem, isto modo quaerens: Quid, si dormiens ille iam sciret quid alius de manu eius

facturus esset, et de industria, plus potus etiam ne expergisceretur, se somno
dederet, ut aliquem iurando falleret; num ei quidquam somnus ad innocentiam
suffragaretur? Quid aliud quam nocentem hominem pronuntiarent ? Quod si
et ille volens vinctus est, ut aliquem similiter praetenta defensione deciperet,
quid ei tandem, ut peccato careat, illa vincula profuerunt? Quanquam his
obstrictus, revera resistere non valeret; sicut ille dormiens, quid tunc fieret,
omnino nesciret. Numquidnam igitur dubitandum est quin peccasse ambo
iudicarentur? Quibus concessis colligerem, nusquam scilicet nisi in voluntate
esse peccatum: cum mihi auxiliaretur etiam illud, quod iustitia peccantes tenet
sola mala voluntate, quamvis quod voluerint implere nequiverint.

13. Quisquamne me ista tractantem, posset dicere, in rebus obscuris abditisque
versari, ubi propter intellegentium paucitatem vel fraudis vel ostentationis
suspicio nasci solet? Secedat paulisper illa intellegibilium sensibiliumque
distinctio: nulla mihi fiat invidia, quod tardas animas subtilium disputationum
stimulis persequor. Liceat mihi me scire vivere, liceat mihi scire me velle vivere:
in quae si consentit genus humanum, tam nobis cognita est voluntas nostra,
quam vita. Neque cum istam scientiam profitemur, metuendum est ne nos
quisquam falli posse convincat: hoc ipsum enim falli nemo potest, si aut non
vivat, aut nihil velit. Non me arbitror quidquam obscurum attulisse, et vereor
ne cuiquam magis, quod haec nimium manifesta sint, videar esse culpandus:
sed quorsum haec tendant, consideremus.

Quid sit voluntas.

14. Non igitur nisi voluntate peccatur. Nobis autem voluntas nostra notissima
est: neque enim scirem me velle, si quid sit voluntas ipsa nescirem. Definitur
itaque isto modo: Voluntas est animi motus, cogente nullo, ad aliquid vel non
amittendum, vel adipiscendum. Cur ergo ita tunc definire non possem? An erat
difficile videre invitum volenti esse contrarium, ita ut contrarium sinistrum
dextro esse dicimus, non ut nigrum albo? Nam eadem res simul et nigra et alba
esse non potest: duorum autem in medio quisque positus, ad alterum sinister
est, ad alterum dexter; simul quidem utrumque unus homo, sed simul
utrumque ad unum hominem nullo modo. Ita quidem invitus et volens unus
animus simul esse potest; sed unum atque idem nolle simul et velle non potest.

Cum enim quisque invitus aliquid facit, si eum roges utrum id facere velit, nolle se dicit: item si roges utrum id velit non facere, velle respondet. Ita invitum ad faciendum, ad non faciendum autem volentem reperies: id est enim unum animum uno tempore habentem utrumque, sed aliud atque aliud ad singula referentem. Cur haec dico? Quia si rursus quaeramus quam ob causam id invitus faciat, cogi se dicet. Nam et omnis invitus faciens cogitur; et omnis qui cogitur, si facit, nonnisi invitus facit. Restat ut volens a cogente sit liber, etiamsi se quisquam cogi putet. Et hoc enim modo omnis qui volens facit, non cogitur; et omnis qui non cogitur, aut volens facit, aut non facit. Haec cum in omnibus hominibus, quos interrogare non absurde possumus, a puero usque ad senem, a ludo litterario usque ad solium sapientis, natura ipsa proclamet; cur ego tunc non viderem in definitione voluntatis ponendum esse: Cogente nullo, quod nunc quasi experientia maiore cautissimus posui? At si hoc ubique manifestum est, et non doctrina, sed natura omnibus promptum; quid restat quod videatur obscurum, nisi forte ullum lateat, aliquid nos velle cum volumus, et ad hoc moveri animum nostrum, idque aut habere nos aut non habere, et si haberemus retinere velle, si non haberemus acquirere? Quare aut non amittere, aut adipisci aliquid vult, omnis qui vult. Quamobrem, si omnia ista luce clariora sunt, sicuti sunt, neque meae tantum, sed notitiae generis humani veritatis ipsius liberalitate donata, cur illo etiam tempore dicere non possem: Voluntas est motus animi, cogente nullo, ad aliquid vel non amittendum, vel adipiscendum?

Peccatum quid.

15. Dicet aliquis: Et hoc te adversum Manichaeos quid adiuvaret? Exspecta; sine prius etiam peccatum definiamus, quod sine voluntate esse non posse omnis mens apud se divinitus conscriptum legit. Ergo peccatum est voluntas retinendi vel consequendi quod iustitia vetat, et unde liberum est abstinere. Quanquam si liberum non sit, non est voluntas. Sed malui grossius quam scrupulosius definire. Etiamne hi libri obscuri mihi scrutandi erant, unde discerem neminem vituperatione suppliciove dignum, qui aut id velit quod iustitia velle non prohibet, aut id non faciat quod facere non potest? Nonne ista cantant et in montibus pastores, et in theatris poetae, et indocti in circulis, et docti in bibliothecis, et magistri in scholis, et antistites in sacratis locis, et in orbe terrarum genus humanum? Quod si nemo vituperatione vel damnatione

dignus est, aut non contra vetitum iustitiae faciens, aut quod non potest non faciens, omne autem peccatum vel vituperandum est, vel damnandum; quis dubitet tunc esse peccatum, cum et velle iniustum est, et liberum nolle; et ideo definitionem illam et veram et ad intellegendum esse facillimam, et non modo nunc, sed tunc quoque a me potuisse dici: Peccatum est voluntas retinendi vel consequendi quod iustitia vetat, et unde liberum est abstinere?

Ex datis definitionibus peccati et voluntatis haeresim Manichaeorum totam evertit.

16. Age nunc, videamus quid nos haec adiuvarent. Plurimum omnino, ut nihil amplius desiderarem: totam quippe causam finirent. Nam quisquis secreta conscientiae suae legesque divinas penitus naturae inditas, apud animum intus, ubi expressiores certioresque sunt, consulens, has duas definitiones voluntatis atque peccati veras esse concedit, totam Manichaeorum haeresim paucissimis et brevissimis, sed plane invictissimis ratiunculis sine ulla cunctatione condemnat. Quod sic considerari potest. Duo animarum genera esse dicunt, unum bonum, quod ita ex Deo sit, ut non ex aliqua materia vel ex nihilo ab eo factum, sed de ipsa eius omnino substantia pars quaedam processisse dicatur, alterum autem malum, quod nulla prorsus ex parte ad Deum pertinere credunt credendumque commendant: et ideo illud summum bonum, hoc vero summum malum esse praedicant: atque ista duo genera fuisse aliquando discreta, nunc esse commixta. Genus quidem commixtionis huius et causam nondum audieram: sed tamen iam quaerere poteram, utrum illud malum genus animarum, antequam bono misceretur, habuisset aliquam voluntatem. Si enim non habebat, sine peccato atque innocens erat, et ideo nullo modo malum. Si autem ideo malum, quia licet esset sine voluntate, tamquam ignis, tamen si bonum attigisset, violaret, atque corrumperet: quantum est nefas, et naturam mali tantum valere ad commutandam ullam Dei partem, et summum illud bonum corruptibile et violabile credere? Quod si voluntas inerat, profecto inerat, cogente nullo, motus animi ad aliquid vel non amittendum, vel adipiscendum. Hoc autem aliquid, aut bonum erat, aut bonum putabatur: non enim aliter appeti posset. Sed in summo malo, ante commixtionem quam praedicant, nullum unquam bonum fuit. Unde igitur ibi vel scientia vel opinio boni esse potuit? An nihil volebant quod apud se esset, atque illud bonum verum, quod extra erat, appetebant? Ista vero praeclara et magna laude praedicanda voluntas

est, qua summum appetitur et verum bonum. Unde igitur in summo malo motus animi tanta laude dignissimus? An studio nocendi appetebant? Primo, eodem revolvitur ratio. Qui enim nocere vult, bono aliquo vult privare alium propter aliquod bonum suum. Erat igitur in eis vel scientia boni, vel opinio, quae summo malo nullo modo esse debebat. Deinde bonum illud extra se positum, cui nocere studebant, utrum omnino esset, unde cognoverant? Si intellexerant, quid tali mente praeclarius? An quidquam est aliud, quo magnis laboribus omnis bonorum porrigatur intentio, nisi ut summum illud et sincerum bonum intellegatur? Quod ergo nunc vix paucis bonis iustisque conceditur, id tunc illud merum malum nullo bono adiuvante iam poterat? Si autem illae animae corpora gerebant, et id oculis viderant; quae linguae, quae pectora, quae ingenia laudandis istis oculis praedicandisque sufficiunt, quibus vix possunt mentes iustorum adaequari? Quanta bona invenimus in summo malo! Si enim videre Deum malum est, non est bonum Deus: bonum est autem Deus: bonum est igitur Deum videre; et nescio quid huic bono comparari queat. Porro quod videre bonum est, unde fieri potest ut posse videre sit malum? Quapropter quidquid vel in illis oculis, vel in istis mentibus fecit, ut ab his possit videri divina substantia, magnum et ineffabili laude dignissimum bonum fecit. Si autem non factum, sed ipsum per se tale ac sempiternum erat, difficile hoc malo quidquam melius invenitur.

Ex malarum item animarum iusta damnatione sequitur non natura, sed voluntate malas esse.

17. Postremo, ut nihil horum laudandorum habeant illae animae, quae illorum rationibus habere coguntur, quaererem utrum aliquas an nullas animas Deus damnet. Si nullas, nullum meritorum iudicium est, nulla providentia et casu potius quam ratione mundus administratur, vel potius non administratur: non enim administratio casibus danda est. Hoc autem si omnibus qualibet religione devinctis credere nefas est, restat ut aut sit aliquarum animarum damnatio, aut nulla peccata sint. Sed si nulla peccata sunt, etiam nullum malum: quod isti si dixerint, haeresim suam uno ictu interficiunt. Convenit igitur mihi cum illis, animas aliquas divina lege iudicioque damnari. At hae, si bonae sint, quae illa iustitia est? Si malae; natura, an voluntate? Sed natura esse malae animae nullo modo queunt. Unde hoc docemus? De superioribus definitionibus voluntatis atque peccati. Quia dicere animas, et esse malas, et nihil peccare, plenum est

dementiae: dicere autem peccare sine voluntate, magnum deliramentum est; et peccati reum tenere quemquam, quia non fecit quod facere non potuit, summae iniquitatis est et insaniae. Quamobrem illae animae quidquid faciunt, si natura, non voluntate faciunt, id est, si libero et ad faciendum et ad non faciendum motu animi carent; si denique his abstinendi ab opere suo potestas nulla conceditur, peccatum earum tenere non possumus. At omnes fatentur, et malas animas iuste, et eas quae non peccaverunt, iniuste damnari: fatentur igitur eas malas esse quae peccant. Illae autem, sicut ratio docuit, non peccant. Animarum ergo malarum genus nescio quod extraneum, quod a Manichaeis inducitur, nullum est.

Animas esse natura bonas, quibus datur venia peccatorum.

18. Nunc bonum illud genus videamus, quod rursus ita laudant, ut ipsam Dei substantiam dicant esse. Quanto autem melius est ut suum ordinem meritumque quisque cognoscat, nec ita sacrilega superbia ventiletur, ut cum se toties commutari sentiat, summi illius boni, quod incommutabile pia ratio profitetur et docet, credat esse substantiam? Ecce enim cum manifestum sit non peccare animas in eo quod non sunt tales, quales esse non possunt; unde constat iam nescio quas illas inductitias nullo modo peccare, et propterea illas omnino non esse: relinquitur, ut quoniam concedunt esse peccata, non inveniant quibus ea tribuant, nisi bono generi animarum et substantiae Dei. Maxime autem urgentur auctoritate christiana: numquam enim negaverunt dari veniam peccatorum, cum fuerit ad Deum quisque conversus; numquam dixerunt (ut alia multa) quod Scripturis divinis hoc quispiam corruptor inseruerit. Quibus ergo peccata donantur? Si alieni generis illis malis, possunt et bonae fieri, possunt Dei regnum possidere cum Christo. Quod isti quia negant, nec habent alterum genus, nisi earum quas de substantia Dei esse perhibent; restat ut non solum etiam ipsas, sed ipsas solas peccare fateantur. Ego autem nihil pugno ne solae peccent: peccant tamen. At enim mali commixtione coguntur? Si ita cogantur, ut resistendi potestas nulla sit, non peccant: si est in potestate sua resistere, et propria voluntate consentiunt, cur tanta bona in summo malo, cur hoc malum in summo bono, per doctrinam illorum cogimur invenire; nisi quia neque illud malum est quod suspicione inducunt, neque hoc summum bonum quod superstitione pervertunt?

Ex deliberatione in malam et in bonam partem non haberi duo animarum genera. Concesso genere animarum illicentium ad turpia, non sequi has esse natura malas, alias esse summum bonum.

19. At si de duobus istis generibus animarum delirare illos et errare docuissem, aut certe ipse didicissem, quid remanere poterat, cur mihi iam de ulla re audiendi vel consulendi viderentur? An ut discerem hinc ostendi animarum duo esse genera, quod in deliberando nunc in malam partem, nunc in bonam nutat assensio? Cur non magis hoc signum est unius animae, quae libera illa voluntate huc et huc ferri, hinc atque hinc referri potest? Nam mihi cum accidit, unum me esse sentio utrumque considerantem, alterutrum eligentem: sed plerumque illud libet, hoc decet, quorum nos in medio positi fluctuamus. Nec mirum: ita enim nunc constituti sumus, ut et per carnem voluptate affici, et per spiritum honestate possimus. Quare non duas animas hinc fateri cogor? Possumus enim melius et multo expeditius intellegere duo genera bonarum rerum, quorum tamen neutrum ab auctore Deo sit alienum, unam animam ex diversis afficere partibus, inferiore ac superiore, vel quod recte ita dici potest, exteriore atque interiore. Ista sunt duo genera, quae sensibilium et intellegibilium nomine paulo ante tractavimus, quae carnalia et spiritalia libentius et familiarius nos vocamus. Sed factum est nobis difficile a carnalibus abstinere, cum panis verissimus noster spiritalis sit. Cum labore namque nunc edimus panem. Neque enim nullo in supplicio sumus peccato transgressionis mortales ex immortalibus facti. Ideo contingit ut cum ad meliora conantibus nobis, consuetudo facta cum carne et peccata nostra quodam modo militare contra nos, et difficultatem nobis facere coeperint, nonnulli stulti aliud genus animarum quod non sit ex Deo superstitione obtusissima suspicentur.

20. Quanquam etiam si eis concedatur inferiore alio genere animarum nos illici ad turpia, non inde conficiunt aut illas natura malas esse, aut istas summum bonum. Fieri enim potest ut propria illae voluntate appetendo quod non licebat, hoc est, peccando, ex bonis factae sint malae; rursusque fieri bonae possint, sed ut fit quamdiu manent in peccato, ad sese alias occulta quadam suasione traducant: deinde, ut omnino malae non sint, sed in suo genere, quamvis inferiore, opus proprium sine ullo peccato exerceant: istae autem superiores quibus actionem longe praestantiorem rerum moderatrix iustitia summa tribuerit, si illas inferiores sequi et imitari voluerint, peccando fiunt

malae, non quia malas, sed quia male imitantur. Ab illis enim agitur proprium, ab istis appetitur alienum: unde illae in suo gradu manent, istae ad inferiora merguntur, velut cum homines ferina sectantur. Pulchre namque incedit quadrupedans equus: at si hoc homo pedibus manibusque imitetur, quis eum vel palearum cibo dignum putet? Recte igitur plerumque improbamus imitantem, cum eum quem imitatur probemus. Improbamus autem, non quia non sit assecutus, sed quia omnino assequi voluit. In equo enim probamus illud, cui quantum praeponimus hominem, tantum offendimur quod inferiora sectatur. Quid inter ipsos homines, in emittenda voce nonne quod praeco bene facit, etiamsi clarius ac melius id faciat senator praecone, insanus est? Coelestia suscipe: lucens luna laudatur, suoque cursu atque vicibus bene considerantibus satis placet; tamen si eam sol velit imitari (fingamus enim eum posse habere huiusmodi voluntates), cui non summe ac iure displiceat? Ex quibus illud est quod intellegi volo. Etiam si sunt animae (quod interim incertum est), corporeis officiis non peccato, sed natura deditae, nosque, quanquam sint inferiores, aliqua tamen interiore vicinitate contingunt, non illas ideo malas haberi oportere, quia et nos cum eas sequimur, et corporea diligimus, mali sumus. Propterea enim corporea diligendo peccamus, quia spiritalia diligere et iustitia iubemur et natura possumus, et tunc in nostro genere optimi et beatissimi sumus.

21. Quamobrem, quid habet argumenti aestuans in utramque partem deliberatio, modo in peccatum prona, modo in recte factum subvecta, ut duo animarum genera, quorum alterius natura ex Deo sit, alterius non sit, cogamur accipere, cum alias tot causas alternantis cogitationis coniicere liceat? Sed haec obscura esse, et incassum ab animis lippientibus quaeri, quisquis bonus rerum existimator est, videt. Quare illa potius quae de voluntate atque peccato dicta sunt, illa, inquam, quae summa iustitia neminem ratione utentem ignorare permittit, illa quae si auferantur nobis, nihil est unde disciplina virtutis inchoetur, nihil unde a vitiorum morte surgatur, etiam atque etiam considerata satis clare ac dilucide Manichaeorum haeresim falsam esse convincunt.

Rursum ex paenitendi utilitate monstratur animas non natura malas esse.

22. Horum simile est quod de poenitendo nunc dicam. Nam, ut inter omnes sanos constat, et quod ipsi Manichaei non solum fatentur, sed et praecipiunt, utile est poenitere peccati. Quid ego nunc in hanc rem divinarum Scripturarum testimonia, quae usquequaque diffusa sunt, colligam? Vox est etiam ista naturae: neminem stultum rei huius notitia deseruit; hoc nobis nisi penitus insitum esset, periremus. Potest aliquis dicere, non se peccare: non autem sibi esse, si peccaverit, poenitendum, nulla barbaries dicere audebit. Quae cum ita sint, quaero ex duobus illis generibus animarum, cuius sit poenitere peccati? Scio quidem neque illius esse posse, qui male facere, neque illius qui bene facere non potest: quare, ut eorum verbis utar, si animam tenebrarum peccati poenitet, non est de substantia summi mali; si animam lucis, non est de substantia summi boni. Poenitendi enim affectus ille qui prodest, et male fecisse poenitentem, et bene facere potuisse testatur. Quomodo igitur ex me nihil mali, si ego perperam feci? aut quomodo me recte poenitet, si ego non feci? Audi partem alteram: Quomodo ex me nihil boni est, cui bona voluntas inest? aut quomodo me recte poenitet, si non inest? Quamobrem aut negent isti esse poenitendi magnam utilitatem, ut non solum a christiano nomine, sed ab omni etiam vel imaginaria ratione pellantur; aut animarum illa duo genera, unum ex quo nihil mali, alterum ex quo nihil boni sit, dicere atque docere iam desinant: quod si faciant, Manichaei esse utique iam desinent; nam tota illa secta ista bicipiti, vel potius praecipiti animarum varietate fulcitur.

23. Ac mihi quidem satis est sic scire quod Manichaei errent, ut scio poenitendum esse peccati: et tamen si nunc amicorum meorum aliquem, qui usque adhuc illos audiendos putat, compellem iure amicitiae, et ei dicam: Scisne utile esse, cum quisque peccaverit, poenitere? sine dubitatione se scire iurabit. Si ergo te fecero ita scire falsam esse Manichaeorum haeresim, desiderabisne amplius? Quid amplius se posse in hac re desiderare respondeat. Bene quidem huc usque. Sed cum ostendere coepero certas necessariasque rationes, quae illam propositionem adamantinis, ut dicitur, catenis innexae consequuntur, remque totam ad conclusionem qua illa evertitur secta perduxero; negabit se forsitan scire utilitatem illam poenitendi, quam nemo doctus, nemo indoctus ignorat; et potius se scire contendet, cum dubitamus et deliberamus, duas in nobis animas patrocinia propria singulis quaestionis partibus adhibere. O consuetudo peccati! o comes poena peccati! Vos me tunc a rerum tam manifestarum consideratione avertistis; sed non sentienti

nocebatis: nunc vero in familiarissimis meis similiter non sentientibus me iam vulneratis torquetisque sentientem.

Orat pro amicis quos habuit erroris socios.

24. Attendite ista, quaeso, carissimi: vestra ingenia bene novi. Si mihi nunc vos qualiscumque hominis mentem rationemque conceditis, multo certiora sunt, quam quae ibi vel videbamur discere, vel magis credere cogebamur. Deus magne, Deus omnipotens, Deus summae bonitatis, quam inviolabilem atque incommutabilem credi atque intellegi fas est, Trina unitas, quam catholica Ecclesia colit, supplex oro, expertus in me misericordiam tuam, ne homines cum quibus mihi a pueritia in omni convictu fuit summa consensio, in tuo cultu a me dissentire permittas. Video maxime exspectari hoc loco, quomodo etiam catholicas Scripturas a Manichaeis accusatas vel tunc defenderem, si, ut dico, cautus essem; vel nunc defendi posse demonstrem. Sed in aliis voluminibus Deus adiuvabit propositum meum; nam huius iam, quantum arbitror, moderata parci sibi postulat longitudo.

The Scriptorium Project is the work of a small group of lay people of various apostolic churches who are interested in the preservation, transmission, and translation of the works of the early and medieval church. Our efforts are to make the works of the church fathers accessible to anyone who might have an interest in Christian antiquities and the theological, philosophical, and moral writings that have become the bedrock of Western Civilization.

To-date, our releases have pulled from the Greek, Syriac, Georgian, Latin, Celtic, Ethiopian, and Coptic traditions of Christianity, and have been pulled from sundry local traditions and languages.

Other Catalogue Titles for the Early Punic Church in North Africa:

Seven Rules by Ticonius the Donatist *(July 2006)*
Letters on the Council of Ephesus by Capreolus of Carthage (Aug. 2007)
The Time of the Barbarians by St. Quoddeusvult of Carthage (Feb. 2009)
3rd Council of Carthage by Gratus of Carthage (Oct. 2010)
4th Council of Carthage by Geneclius of Carthage (Nov. 2010)
5th Council of Carthage by St. Aurelius of Carthage (Dec. 2010)
The Two Souls of the Manicheans by St. Augustine of Hippo (Jan. 2011)
Two Letters from Byzantine Africa by Licinianus of Carthage (Oct. 2016)
Apology to Gunthamund, King of Vandals by Blossius Aemilius Dracontius (Feb. 2018)
Letter to Pope Theodore by Victor of Carthage (Feb. 2020)
Council of Mileum by St. Aurelius of Carthage (Aug. 2022)
Council of Zella by Donatianus of Zella (Sept. 2022)
Against Palladius the Arian by Vigilius of Thapsus (Nov. 2023)
Response Against Arians by St. Fulgentius of Ruspe (Jan. 2024)
The Final Letter to Latin North Africa by Pope Leo IX (Mar. 2024)
Letters & Pamphlets by Fulgentius Ferrandus (Apr. 2024)